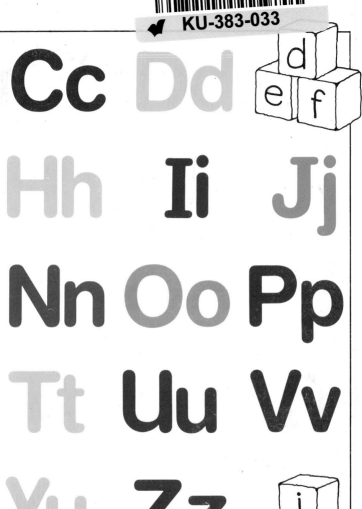

Cc Dd

Hh Ii Jj

Nn Oo Pp

Tt Uu Vv

Yy Zz

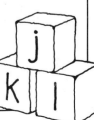

Learning Points

This simple, colourful book helps children to learn to recognise the letters of the alphabet by pairing each letter with an appealing, familiar object.

- As you look at the book together, encourage your child to say the sound of the letter rather than its name (that is, **a** as in *apple* rather than **a** as in *age*).

- Talk about the pictures – does she like apples? Where has he seen an elephant? What are the colours on the parrot's wing?

- Play I-spy at home and on trips out. Remember to use the letter sound.

Acknowledgment
The publishers would like to thank GCP Ltd
for supplying the soft letters used on the cover of this book.

Ladybird books are widely available, but in case of
difficulty may be ordered by post or telephone from:

Ladybird Books – Cash Sales Department
Littlegate Road Paignton Devon TQ3 3BE
Telephone 0803 554761

A catalogue record for this book is available
from the British Library

Published by Ladybird Books Ltd Loughborough Leicestershire UK
Ladybird Books Inc Auburn Maine 04210 USA

alphabet

illustrated by LIZ ANTILL

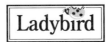

a

apple

ball

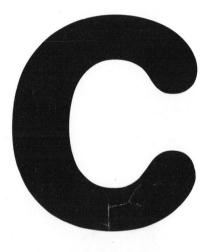

cat

d

duck

e

elephant

f

fish

goat

h

house

ink

jam

kite

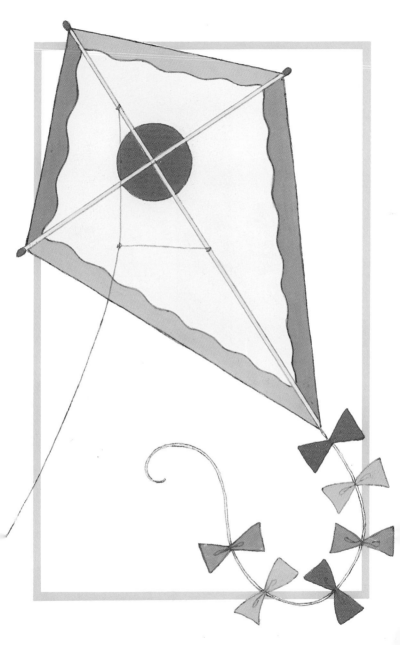

ladder

m

mouse

n
nest

o
orange

parrot

queen

r

rainbow

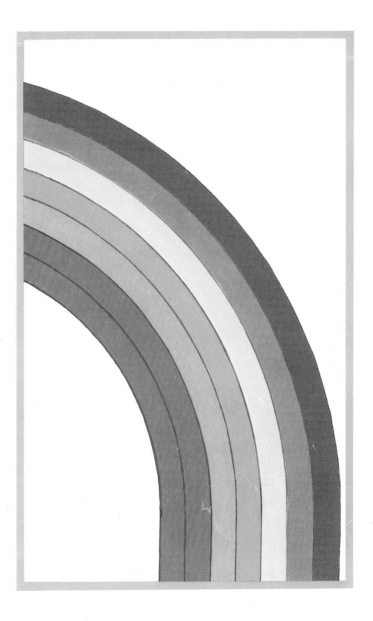

sun

t

tiger

u

umbrella

V

violin

W

watch

x-ray

x as in box

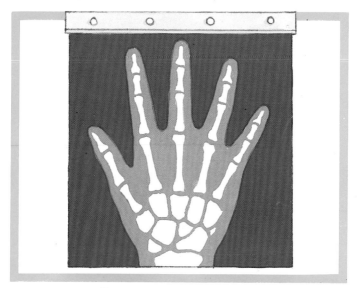

y

yo-yo

z

zebra